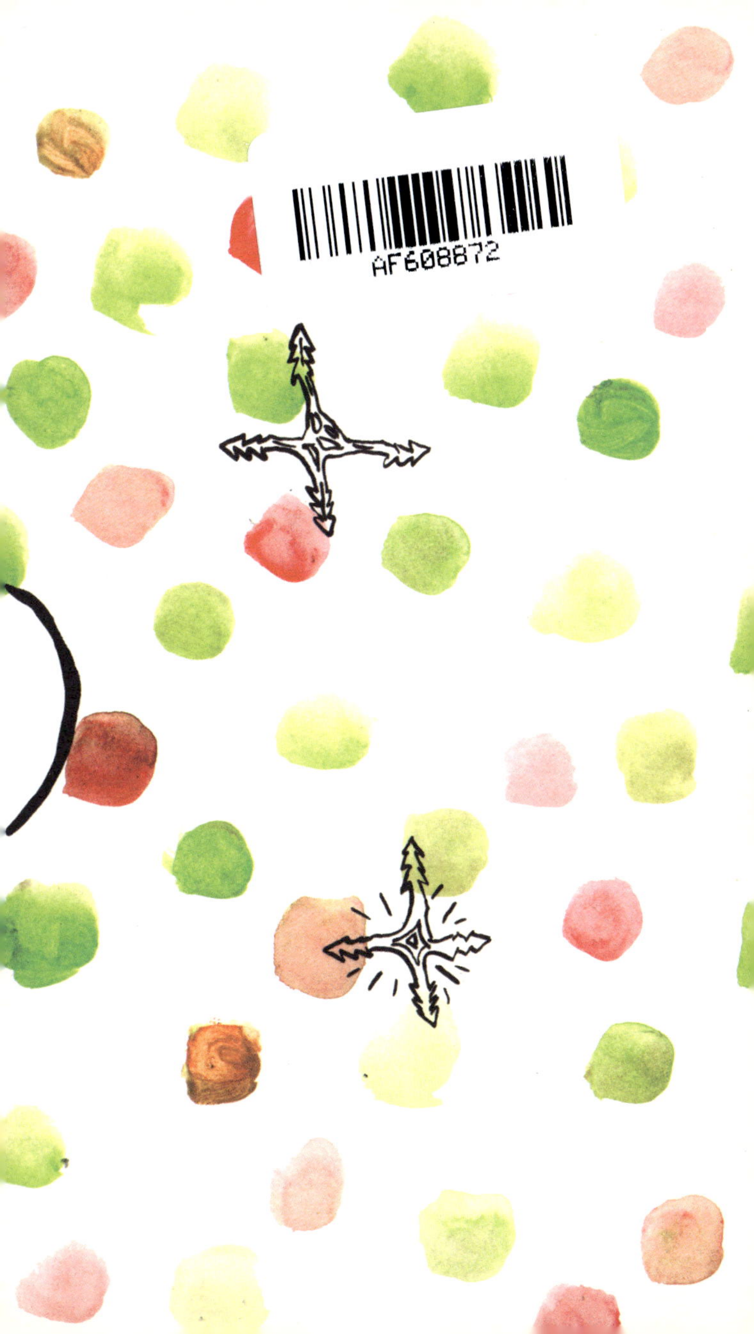
AF608872

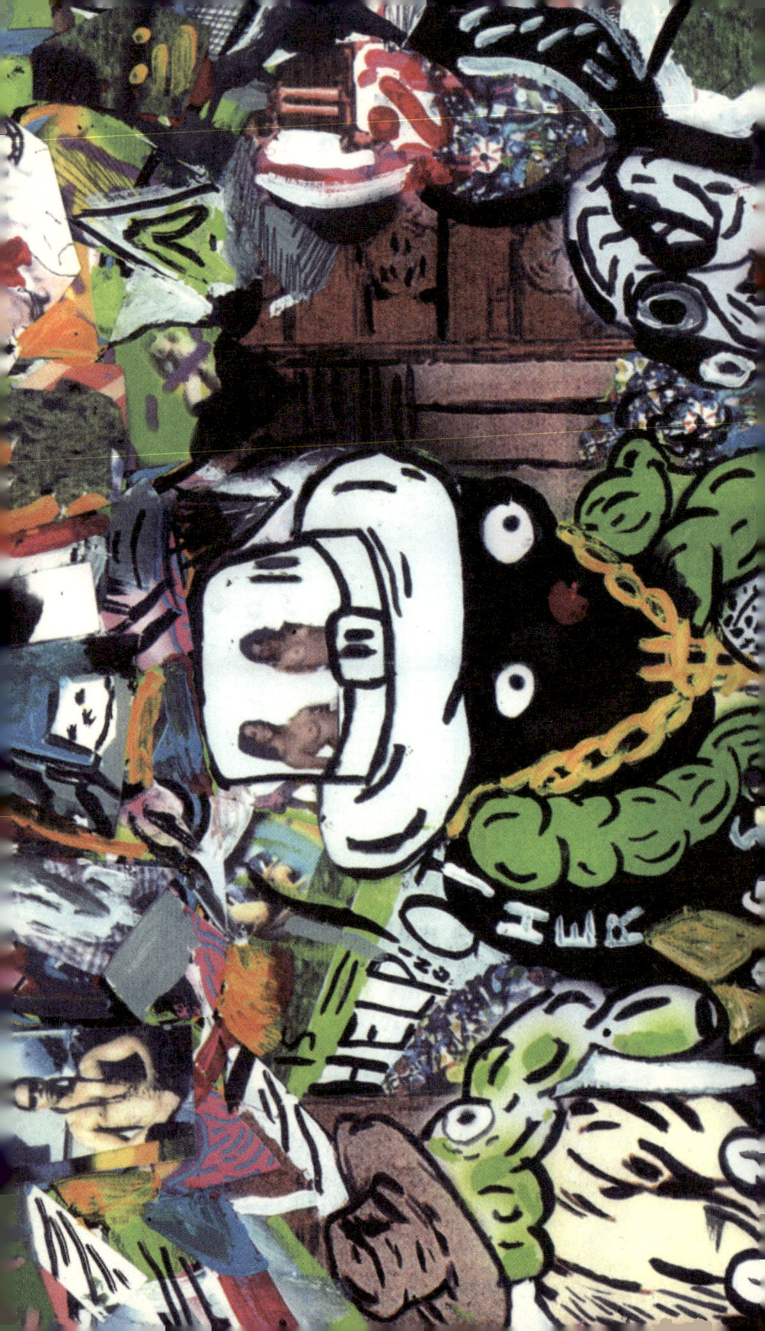

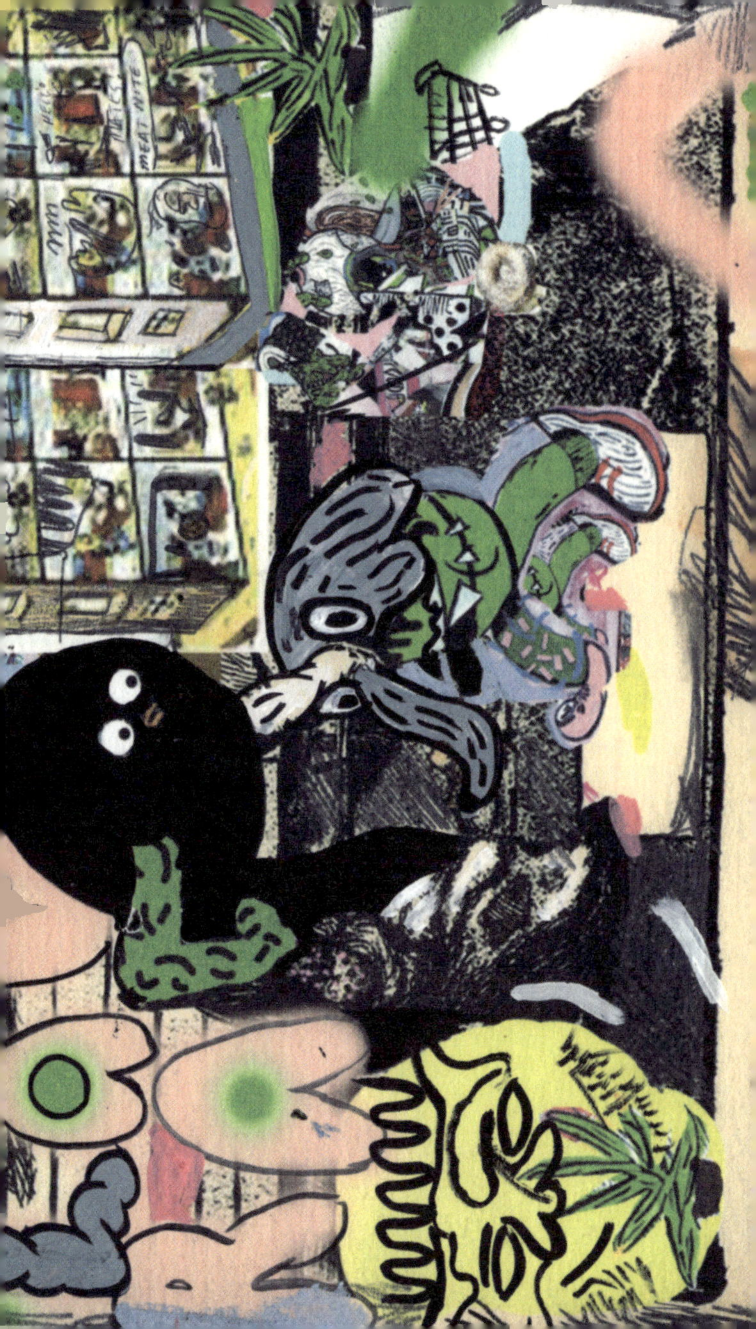

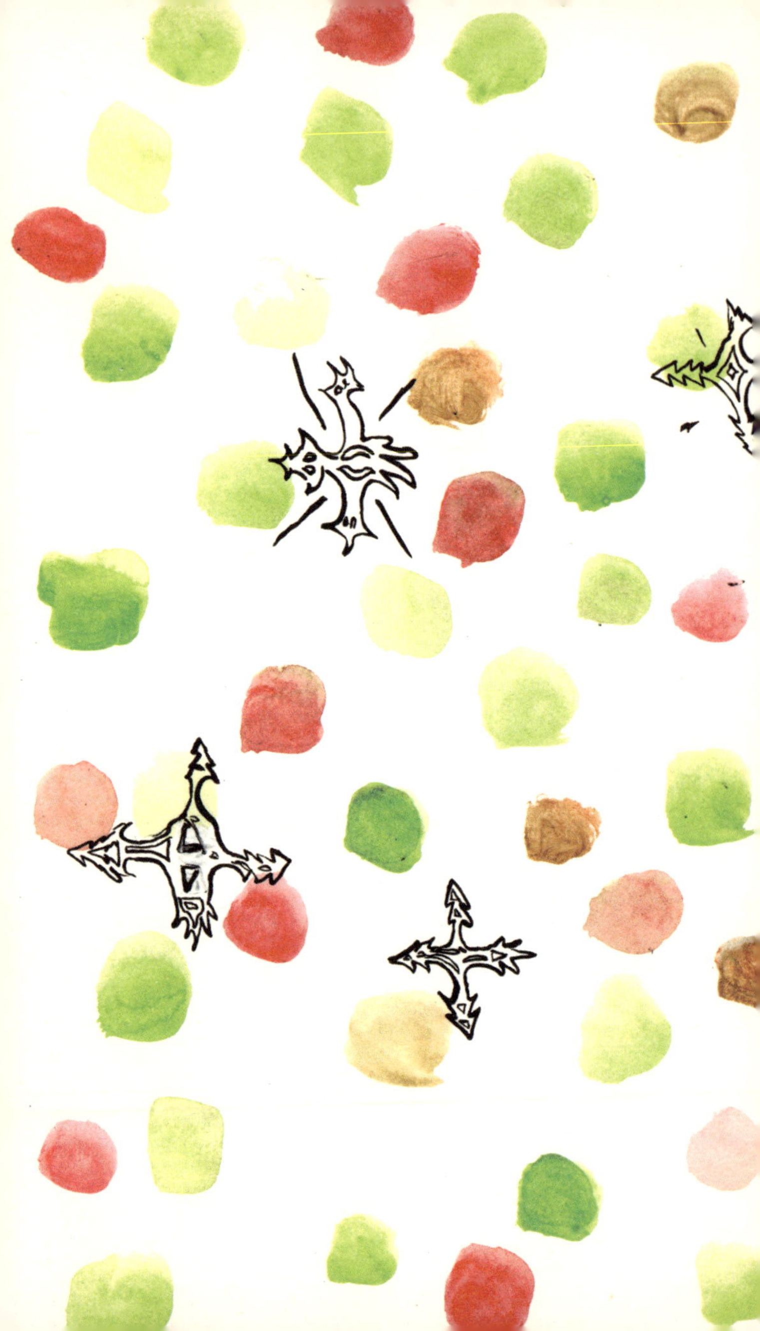

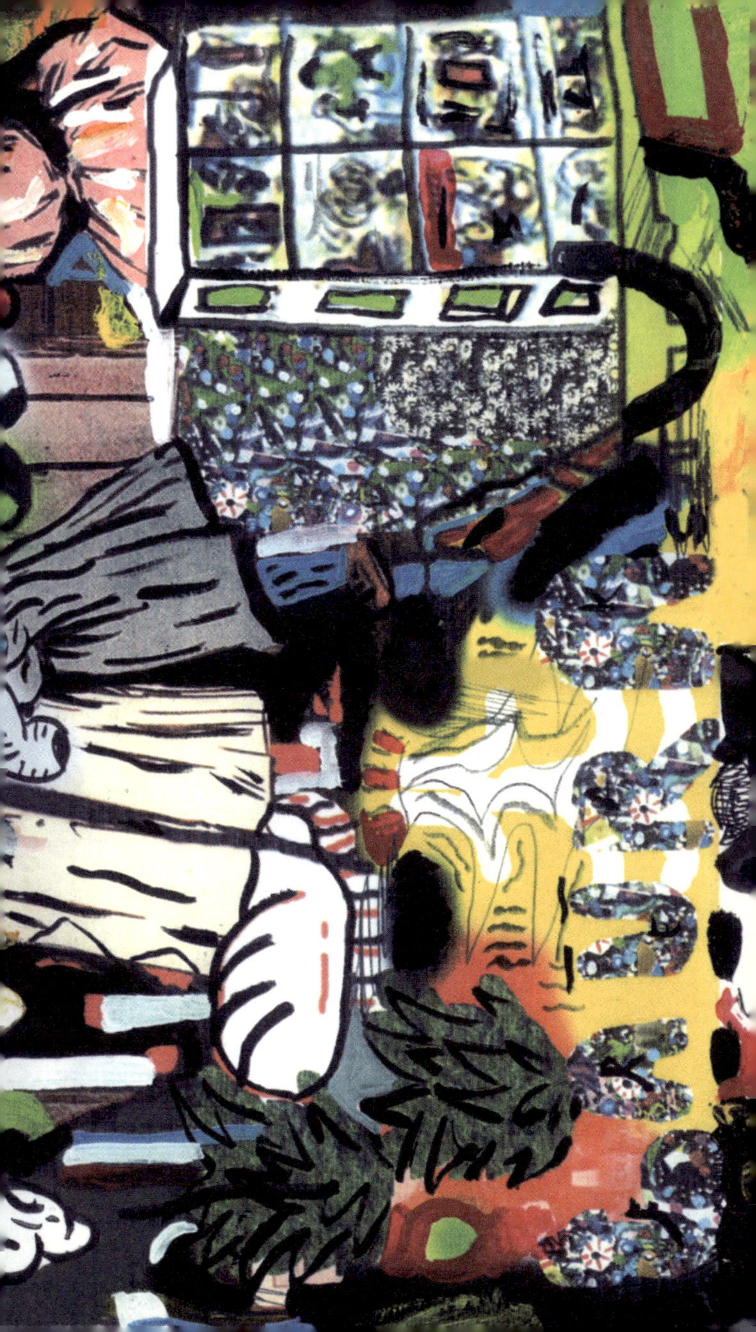

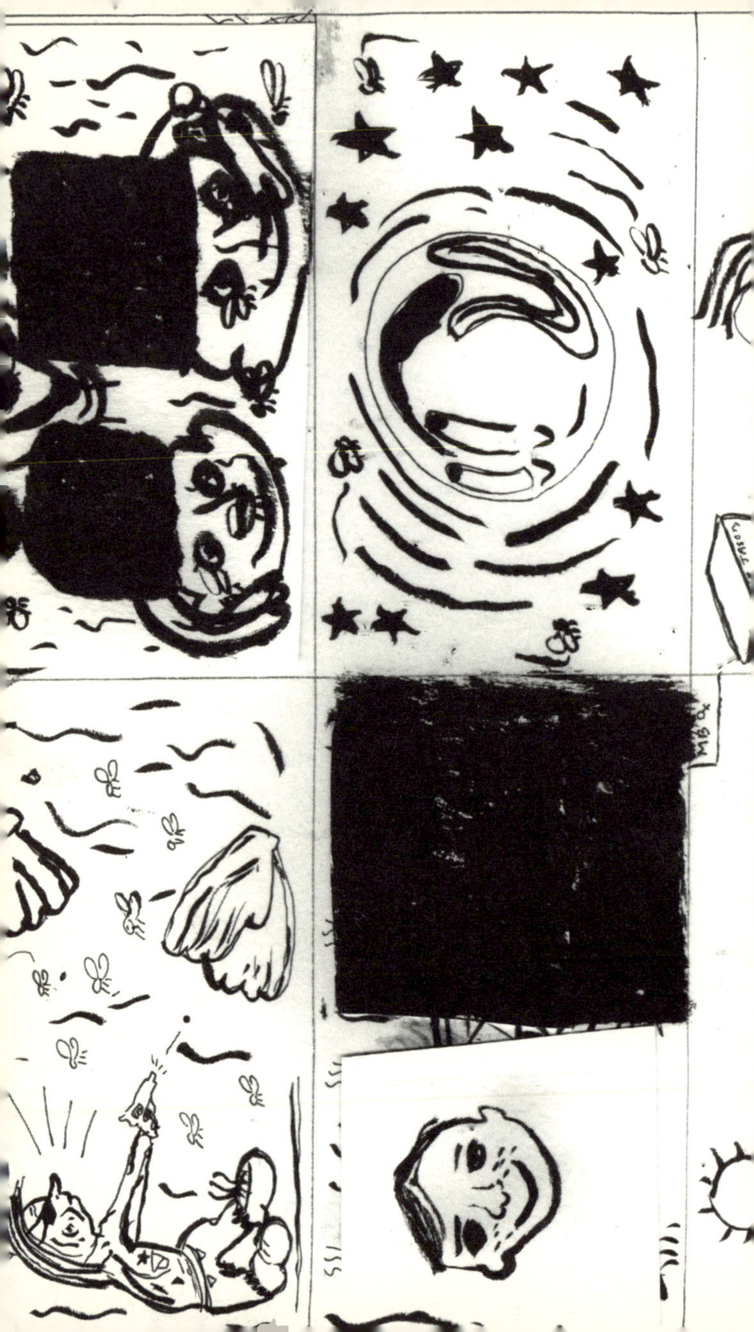

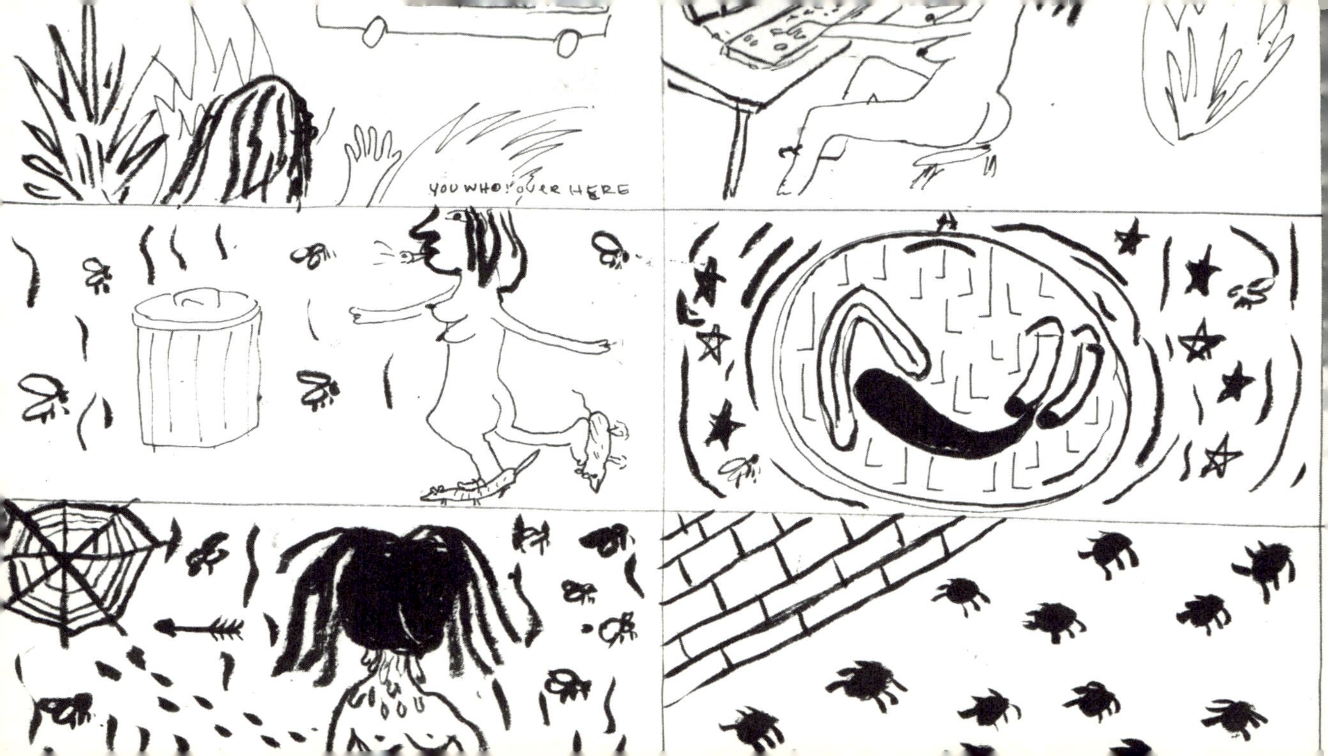
YOU WHO! OVER HERE

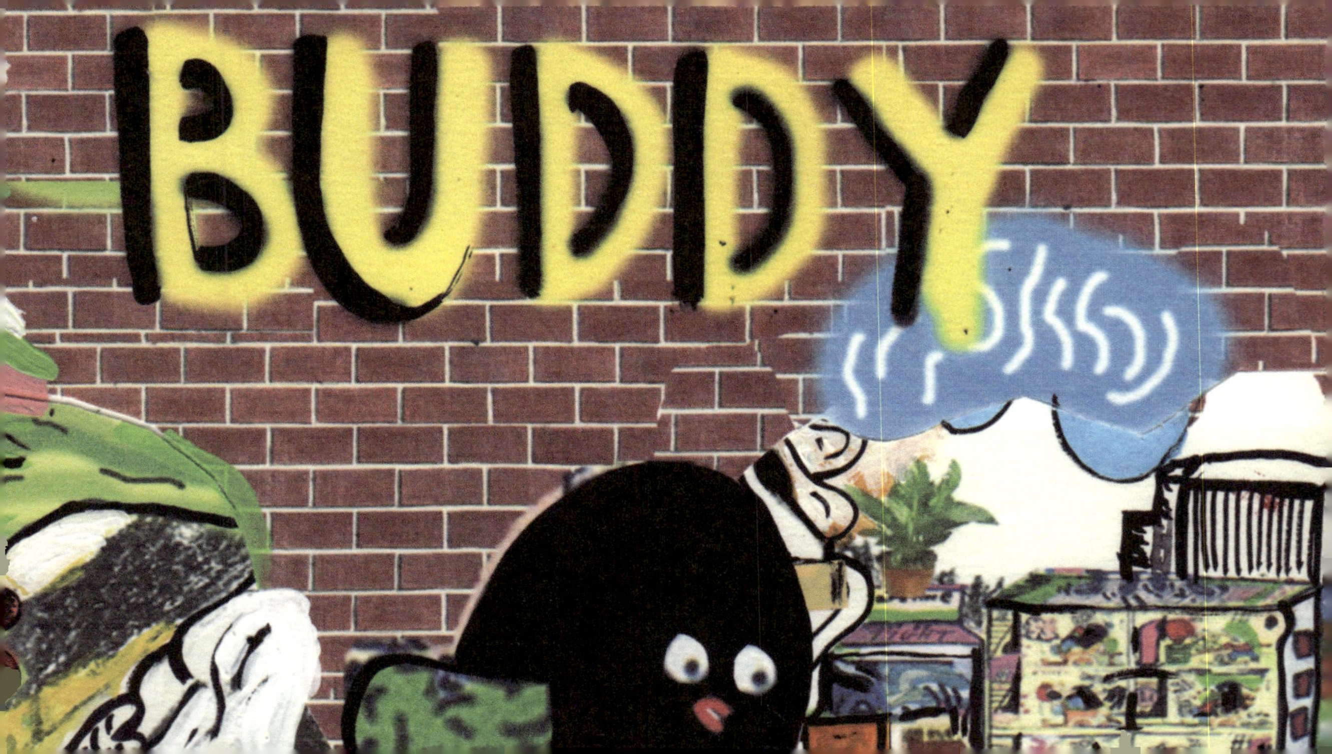
BUDDY

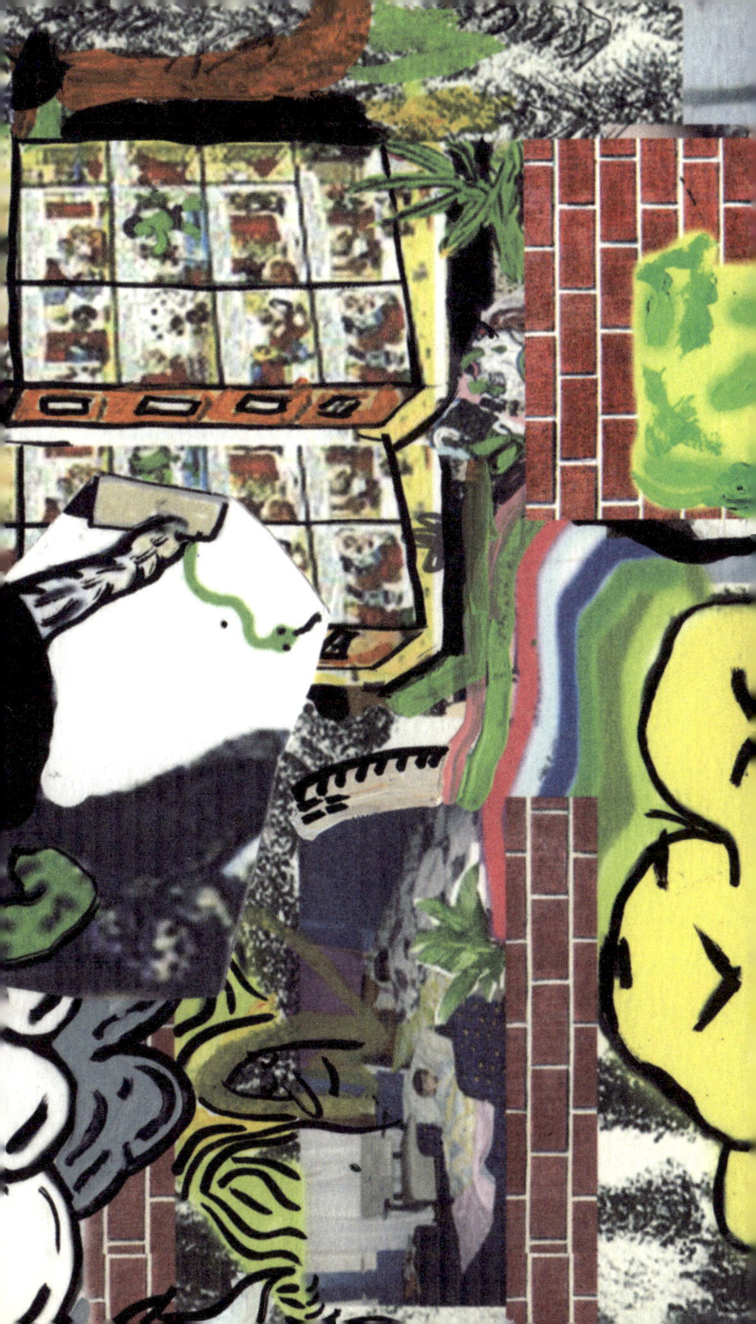

Mark DeLong
Melanie Sheepwash
www.bambi.org.uk

First Edition

Published by Nieves
www.nievesbooks.com

Reproduction without permission prohibited.
All rights reserved. © 2007 Mark DeLong and Nieves

ISBN 978-3-905714-26-5

Jason McLean
Melanie Sheepwash
www.jasonmclean.com

First Edition

Published by Nieves
www.nievesbooks.com

Reproduction without permission prohibited.
All rights reserved. © 2007 Jason McLean and Nieves

ISBN 978-3-905714-26-5

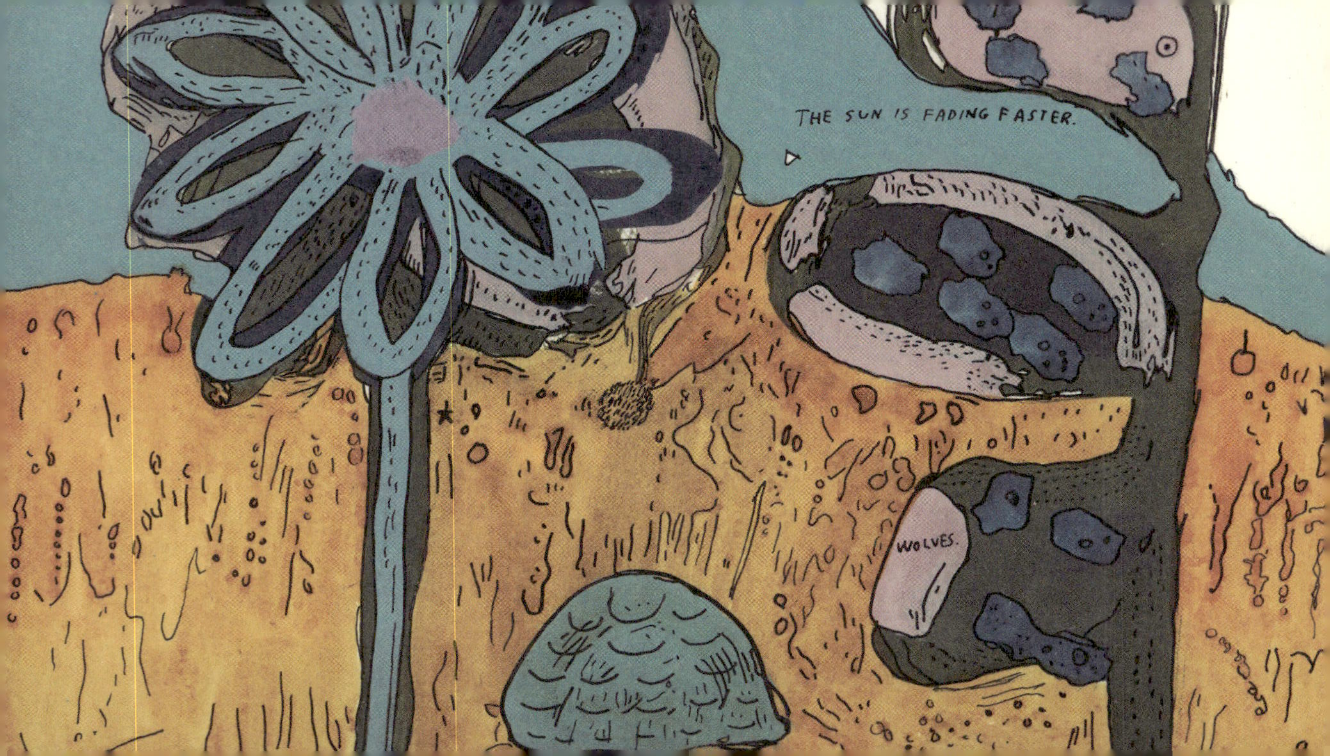
THE SUN IS FADING FASTER.
WOLVES.

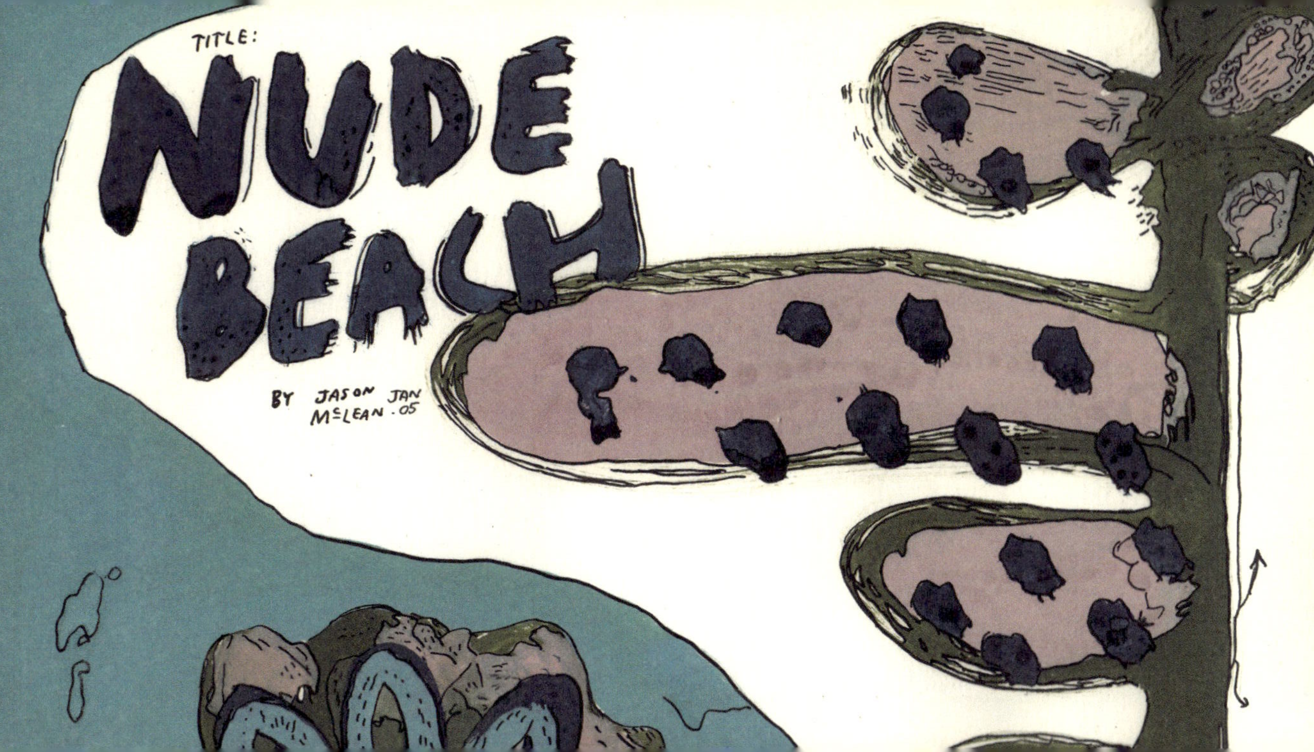
TITLE:
NUDE BEACH
BY JASON JAN
McLEAN .05

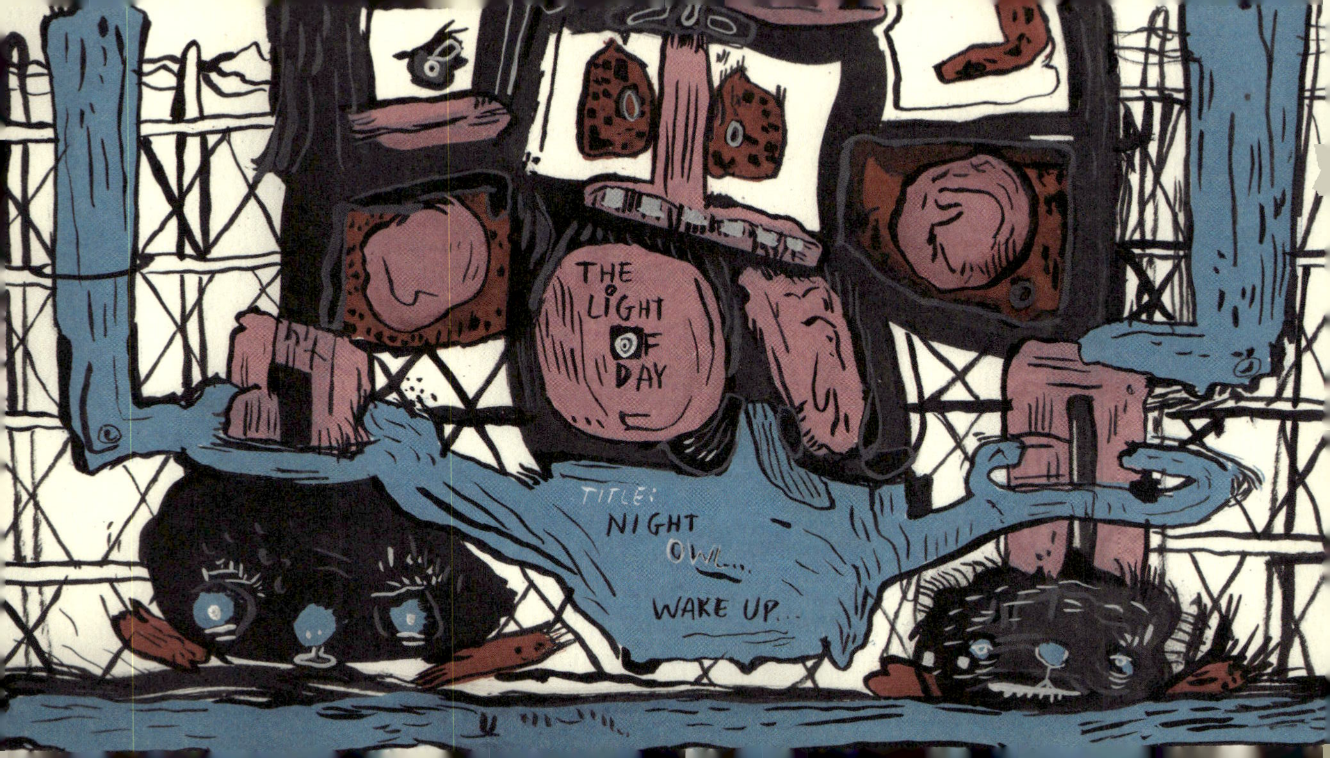
THE LIGHT OF DAY
TITLE:
NIGHT OWL...
WAKE UP...

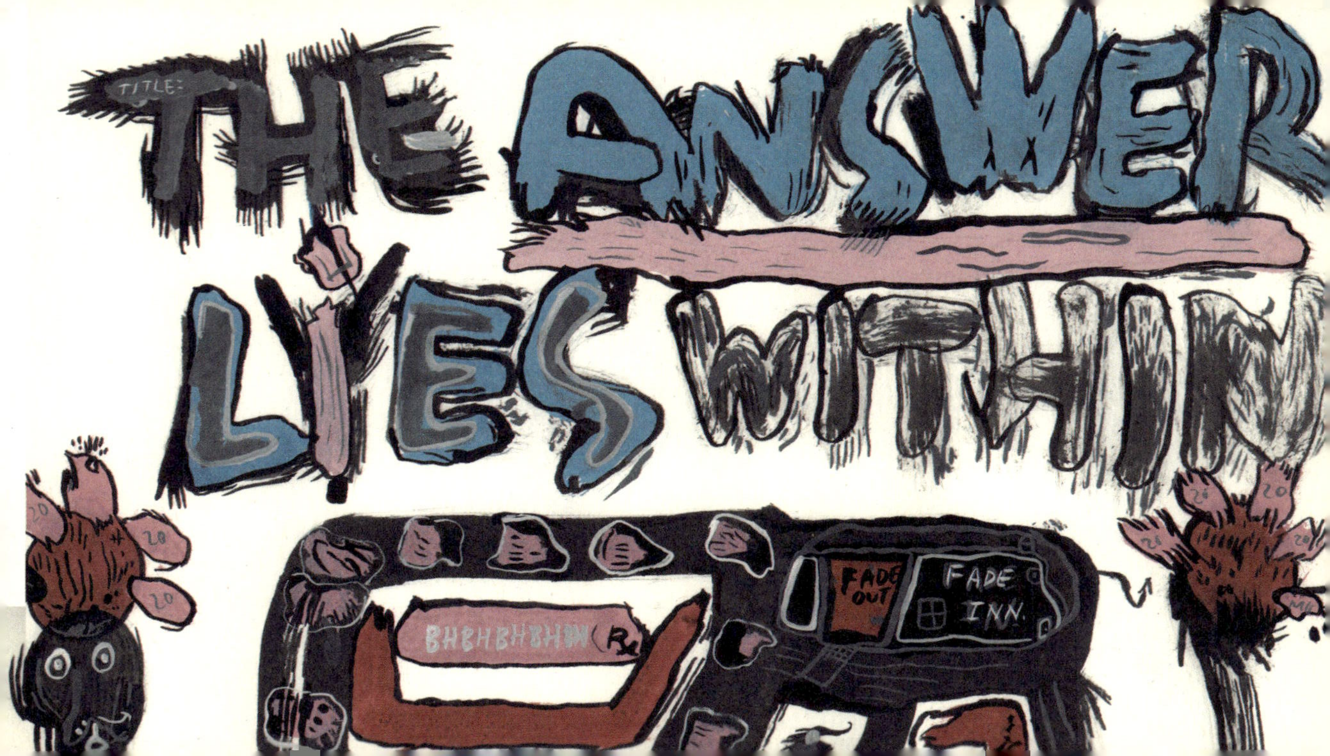

TITLE:
THE ANSWER LIES WITHIN
BHBHBHBHW
FADE OUT
FADE INN.

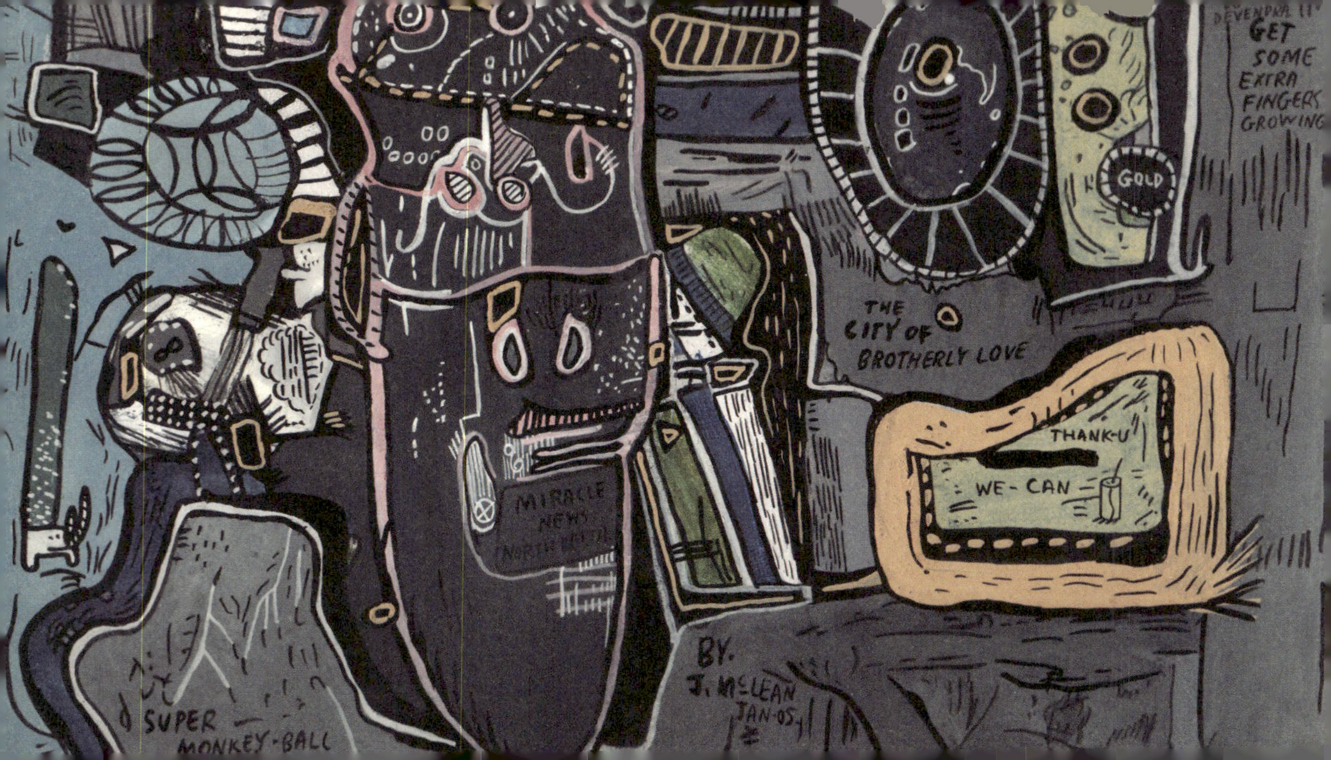

GET SOME EXTRA FINGERS GROWING
GOLD
THE CITY OF BROTHERLY LOVE
THANK-U
WE - CAN
MIRACLE NEWS
SUPER MONKEY-BALL
BY. J. McLEAN JAN-05

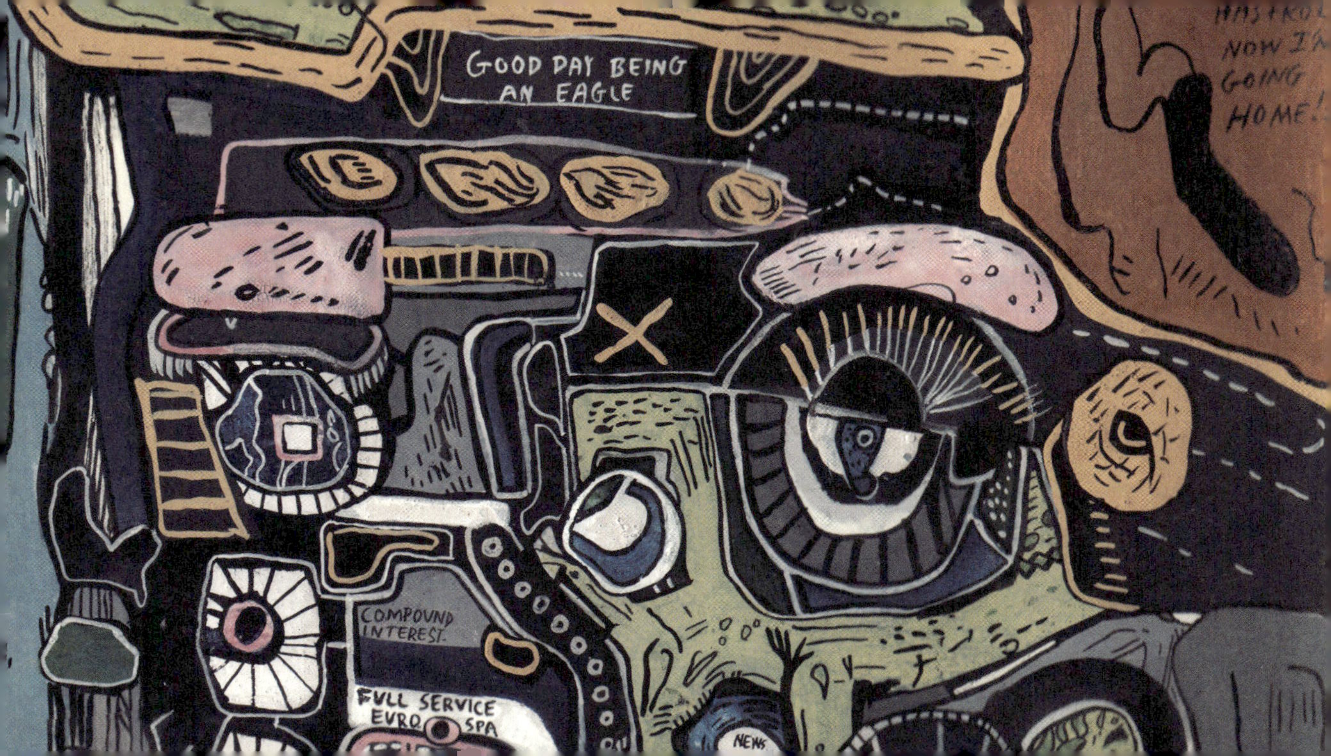
GOOD DAY BEING AN EAGLE
NOW I'M GOING HOME!
COMPOUND INTEREST
FULL SERVICE EURO SPA
NEWS

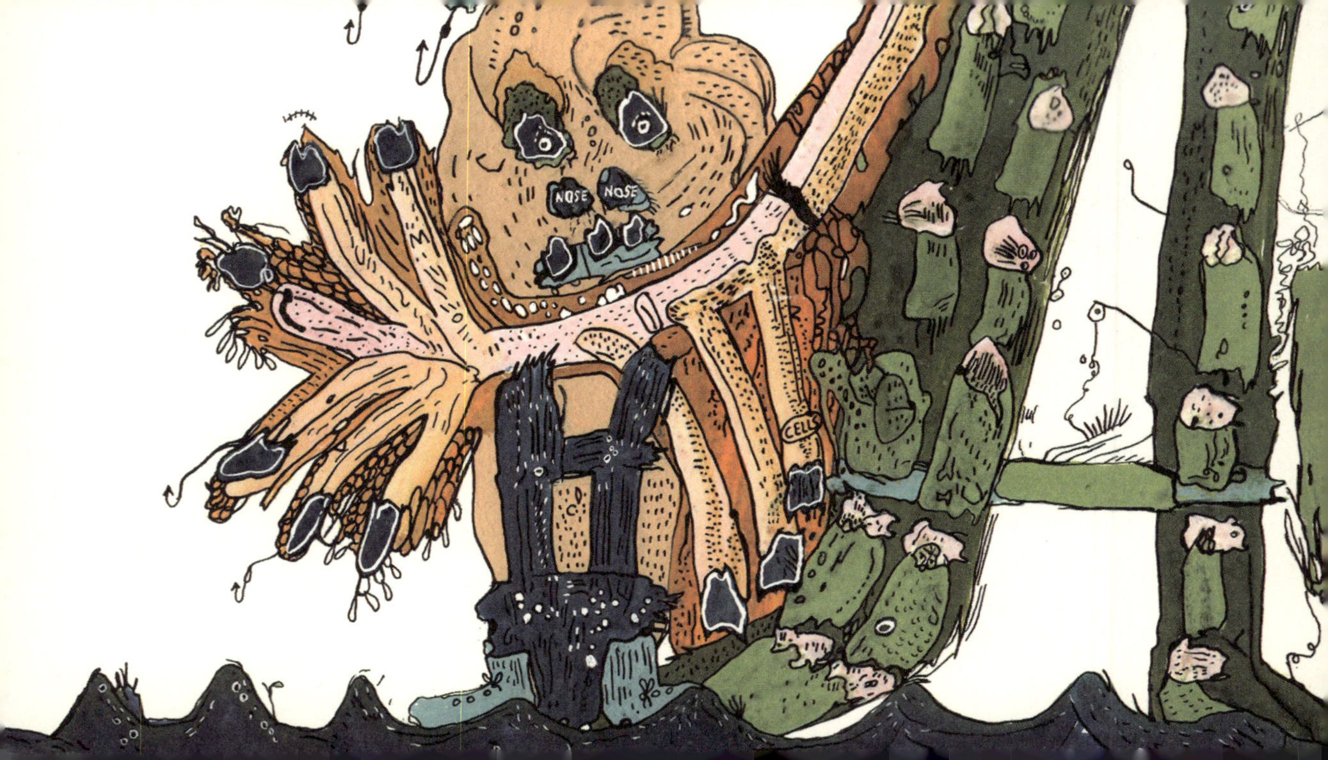
NOSE
NOSE
CELLS

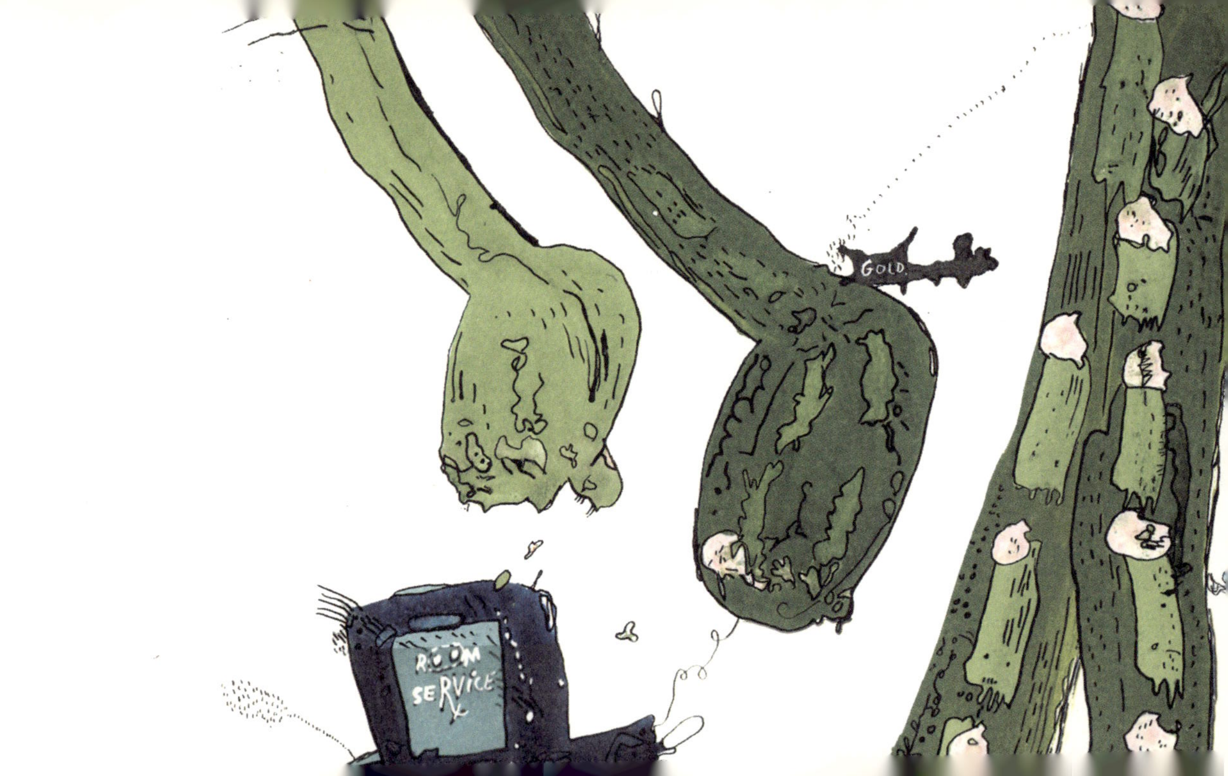
GOLD.
ROOM SERVICE

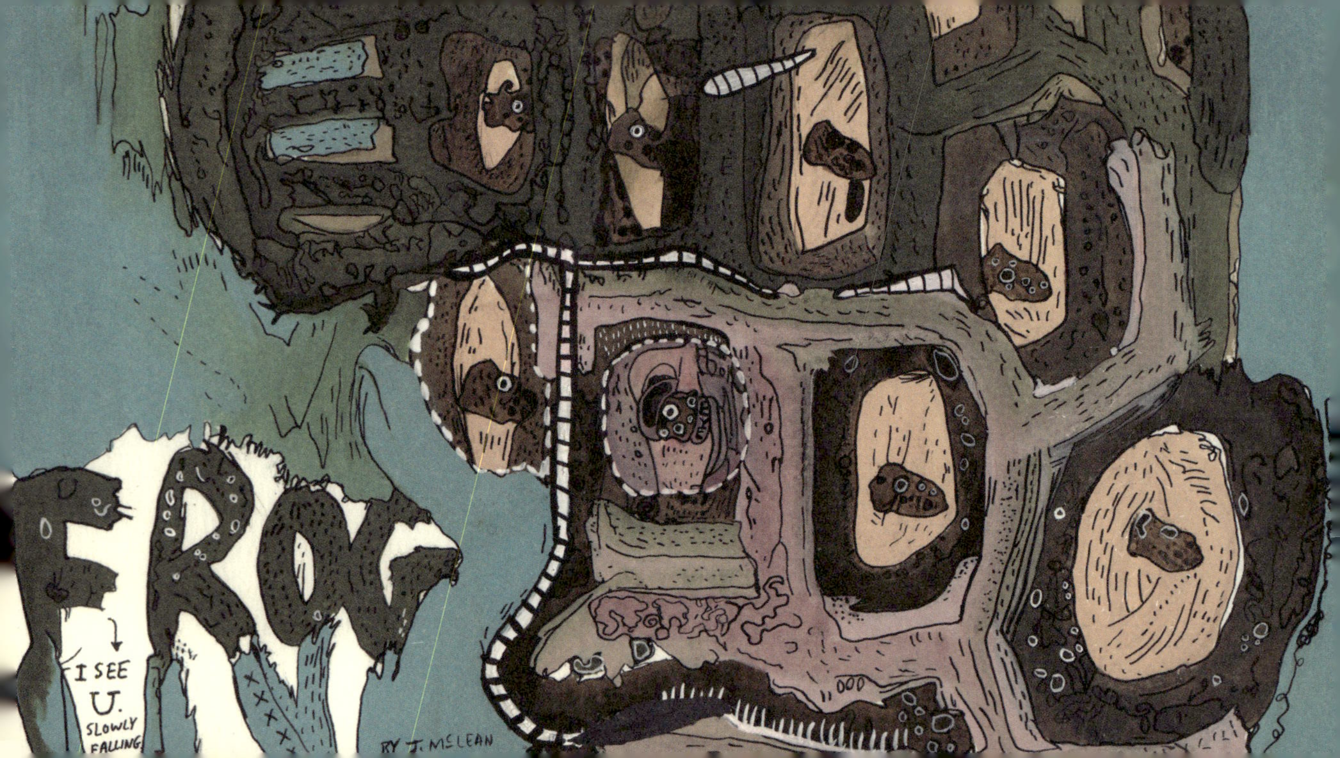
FROG
I SEE U. SLOWLY FALLING
BY J. McLEAN